C.A.N.T.

C.A.N.T.

CHANGE ATTITUDE NOW FOR TOMORROW'S SUCCESS

Jan Murphy

Changing Your Mind-Set for Financial Success

ISBN-13: 9780997251500
ISBN-10: 0997251506
Library of Congress Control Number: 2016904678
Kalamazoo, MI 49001

DEDICATION

This book is dedicated to my beloved mother, Ruby Jean, who is the reason that I am a strong, independent, and confident woman.

To my four children, whom I love with all my heart and soul. I hope to leave a legacy for you to follow.

TABLE OF CONTENTS

I'M JUST AVERAGE.

Introduction: I'm just Average

I'm just an average person who has had above average success. There are probably millions of books about how to achieve wealth and success written by people who have built great wealth. I like reading those books and I get extremely motivated when I read them written by those millionaires.

The truth is most people will never achieve the success and wealth that these above average people enjoy. This book was written to help the average Joe and Jane. People just like me.

There's nothing wrong with not becoming a millionaire nor is it to dream becoming a millionaire. For most people, they're striving for financial security while achieving happiness and good health. For some, that's enough and for others, it's not. What's not good enough for most is living paycheck to paycheck, foregoing vacations or living a lifestyle beyond their means through credit card debt.

Success is just a mindset and if you can convince yourself to take action, I believe that you can achieve the success that you want if you stop listening to everyone around you and start planning for success.

This book is designed to help people who are working the average nine to five job who want more out of their careers and for those who want to build successful businesses.

In this book, you will determine whether or not you have an employee mindset or an entrepreneurial mindset. I belief that the people who achieve the most in this world, have an entrepreneurial mindset and not the employee mindset. It makes no difference if you are trying to achieve success in the corporate world or the business world, your mindset is the key to achieving the success that you want. Don't let others define success for you. Its different things for different people.

So when you read this book, keep in mind it's written for those who want more in life which is achieved by working smarter and sometimes harder than anyone else.

"Believe you can and you're half way there."

- Theodore Roosevelt

THE POWER OF BELIEF

CHAPTER 1

THE POWER OF BELIEF

O*ne* can be a lonely number, but it can be a powerful one! If you have unrelenting enthusiasm and tireless determination in the belief that you can make a difference, you may have a greater impact on the world than you might imagine. Anything is possible.

Some of the most important inventions in history came from people who had a strong belief that they could make a difference and change the world. Most likely, they didn't start out thinking that they were going to impact mankind as they did. The truth is that many of the early inventors were ordinary people with a good idea. Quite frankly, a few were laughed at and scorned, and people didn't think much of their ideas.

Two examples of relentless determination come from Thomas Edison, who discovered electricity, and Alexander Graham Bell, who changed how we communicate with one another by inventing the telephone. Each invention has led to many others. Where would we be today without our cell phones had it not been for Bell? Think about how radio, television, the light bulb, computers, and the Internet have changed the lives of mankind. There have been countless medical discoveries and inventions that save lives every day. Look at the impact that Steve Jobs, a college dropout, had on the world. If it wasn't for these forward-thinking people, where would our society be today?

"It doesn't matter how many times you fail. It doesn't matter how many times you almost get it right. No one is going to know or care about your failures, and neither should you. All you have to do is learn from them and those around you because all that matters in business is that you get it right once. Then everyone can tell you how lucky you are."

— *Mark Cuban, owner of the Dallas Mavericks, cofounder of Broadcast.com, and founder of HDNet*

MISTAKES ARE A NATURAL PROCESS

CHAPTER 2

MISTAKES ARE A NATURAL PROCESS

No one likes to make mistakes, and we all have made our share of them, but the difference between those who succeed and those who do not is their level of persistence, determination, and discipline. People who succeed perceive mistakes as part of a learning curve and a natural process of moving forward. Mistakes should not be misconstrued as failure.

The difference between those who fail and those who succeed is that those who fail quit trying. Failing over and over does not mean that you are a failure; most top performers have perfected their skills through making mistakes over and over; the difference in top athletes and top performers is that they do not dwell on their mistakes.

"It is impossible to live without failing at something, unless you live so cautiously that you might as well not have lived at all, in which case you have failed by default."

- J. K. Rowling

FAMOUS FAILURES
A FEW WHO DID NOT GIVE UP

CHAPTER 3
A Few Who Did Not Give Up

- As a young man, Abraham Lincoln went to war as a captain and returned home as a private. Afterward, he was a failure as a businessman. As a lawyer in Springfield, Illinois, he was too impractical and temperamental to be a success. He turned to politics and was defeated in his first try for the legislature, again defeated in his first attempt to be nominated for Congress, defeated in his application to be commissioner of the General Land Office, defeated in the senatorial election of 1854, defeated in his efforts for the vice-presidency in 1856, and defeated in the senatorial election of 1858. At about that time, he wrote in a letter to a friend, ""I am now the most miserable man living. If what I feel were equally distributed to the whole human family, there would not be one cheerful face on the earth." Lincoln went on to become one of the most admired presidents of modern times.

- Winston Churchill failed sixth grade. He was subsequently defeated in every election for public office until he became prime minister at the age of sixty-two. He later wrote, "Never give in, never give in, never, never, never, never—in nothing, great or small, large or petty—never give in except to convictions of honor and good sense. Never, Never, Never, Never give up." (*His* capitals, mind you.)

- Thomas Edison's teachers said he was "too stupid to learn anything." He was fired from his first two jobs for being "non-productive." As an inventor, Edison made one thousand unsuccessful attempts at inventing the light bulb. When a reporter asked, "How did it feel to fail one thousand times?" Edison replied, "I didn't fail one thousand times. The light bulb was an invention with one thousand steps."

- Albert Einstein did not speak until he was four years old and did not read until he was seven. His parents thought he was "subnormal," and one of his teachers described him as "mentally slow, unsociable, and adrift forever in foolish dreams." He was expelled from school and was refused admittance to the Zurich Polytechnic School. Of course, we all know he did eventually learn to speak and read—even do a little math. Because Einstein is considered the greatest genius of all time, scientists are studying his brain to try to determine whether he was born that way or developed his intellect and trained his brain.

- When Bell Telephone was struggling to get started, its owners offered all their rights to Western Union for $100,000. The offer was rejected with the pronouncement, "What use could this company make of an electrical toy?"

- An expert once said of Vince Lombardi: "He possesses minimal football knowledge and lacks motivation." Lombardi would later write, "It's not whether you get knocked down; it's whether you get back up."

- Michael Jordan and Bob Cousy were each cut from their high school basketball teams. Jordan once stated, "I've failed over and over again in my life. That is why I succeed."

- Walt Disney was fired by a newspaper editor because "he lacked imagination and had no good ideas." He went bankrupt several times before he built Disneyland. In fact, the proposed park was rejected by the city of Anaheim on the grounds that it would only attract riffraff.

- Decca Records turned down a recording contract with the Beatles, saying, "We don't like their sound. Groups of guitars are on their way out." After Decca rejected the Beatles, Columbia records followed suit.

- In 1954, Jimmy Denny, manager of the Grand Ole Opry, fired Elvis Presley after one performance. He told Presley, "You ain't goin' nowhere, son. You ought to go back to drivin' a truck."

- Susan Blakely, owner of Spanx and one of the first self-made female billionaires, launched her business with only $10,000 and had been turned down so many times before finally succeeding!

You are never too old to start a new business or dream a dream or reinvent yourself. Mary Kay Ash, founder of the cosmetic empire, started her company in her midforties. At age sixty-five and on social security, Colonel Harlan Sanders traveled all over the country trying to sell his chicken recipe to restaurants. He slept in his car and looked for someone to back him in his business. He was rejected 1,009 times before someone said yes. And of course, we have all heard the story of Sam Walton, who opened his first Walmart store at the age of forty-five.

Imagine what our world would be like if these people had not believed in themselves and had the determination to keep pursuing their dreams as well as a strong desire to make a difference.

These examples of famous people are only a tiny fraction of those who have achieved success through hard work, determination, and fortitude.

"Action is the foundational key to all success."

- Pablo Picasso

FOUR TRAITS OF SUCCESSFUL PEOPLE

CHAPTER 4
FOUR TRAITS OF SUCCESSFUL PEOPLE

There have been many books written on this topic, but there are four main traits of successful people that most research supports:

Four Main Elements

- Clarity regarding life goals
- Understanding of what they seek to build
- Determination
- Persistence

When I consult with people, I always ask them how passionate they are about what they do. Is it something that they really enjoy doing? Sometimes your passion becomes your obsession. If you cannot wait to get up in the mornings to start your workday, that's enjoying what you do. If you dread getting up and do not look forward to the day, you should reevaluate what you're doing.

You must have a clear vision of what it is that you want out of life and how you are going to get it.

You must stay determined and persistent, but that does not mean that you never have to reinvent yourself or have to refocus. If you stay focused on your goals, the path you take may change. You may find that the direction where you started is not the same direction where you may end up.

"Successful people are simply those with successful habits."

- Brian Tracy

HABITS

CHAPTER 5

HABITS

What do habits have to do with success? Before I answer that question, let's look at how long it takes to form a habit.

Many people believe that it takes twenty-one days to form a habit. This idea was presented in a book published in 1960 by a plastic surgeon, Dr. Maxwell Maltz, who noticed that amputees took, on average, twenty-one days to adjust to the loss of a limb, and he argued that people take twenty-one days to adjust to any major life change.

The University of London studied ninety-six students to find out how long it would take to form a habit by eating a piece of fruit every day at lunch or taking a fifteen-minute run each day. Although the average was sixty-six days, there was marked variation in how long habits took to form: anywhere from eighteen days up to 254 days in the habits examined in this study. As you'd imagine, eating a piece of fruit every day became automatic very quickly, but running for fifteen minutes every day required more discipline. The researchers also noted that

- missing a single day did not reduce the chance of forming a habit;
- a subgroup took much longer than others to form their habits, perhaps suggesting some people are "habit-resistant"; and
- other types of habits may well take much longer.

Forming a habit depends on the difficulty of it, and the difficulty is based on how each individual perceives it. In other words, there are some people who will adapt more quickly to forming a habit whiles others will take longer. A habit becomes an automatic behavior pattern. For example, I dislike running so I imagine that it would take me longer to form the habit to run than it would be for someone who already walks every day and enjoys the outdoors.

In *The Common Denominator of Success*, by E. M. Gray, he found through his research that "the successful person has the habit of doing the things that others do not like to do. Successful people do not necessarily like doing them either, but they subordinate their dislikes to the strength of their purpose."

Ninety percent of what we do is a habit. Our daily routine is a habit. For people to be successful, they must stay on course and identify which habits are necessary to reach their goals. Discipline and commitment are both necessary to keeping us on track in reaching our goals.

"Long-term, we must begin to build our internal strengths. It isn't just skills like computer technology. It's the old-fashioned basics of self-reliance, self-motivation, self-reinforcement, self-discipline, self-command."

- Steven Pressfield

TWENTY-TWO DAYS
TO AUTOMATIC

CHAPTER 6
TWENTY-TWO DAYS TO AUTOMATIC

After providing research data that reflects sixty-six days as a minimum to form a habit, why would I be teaching twenty-two days to form a habit? The twenty-two days is not based on the habit theory but is based on the average number of workdays in a month. Most businesses in the United States operate on a five-day work-week unless it's a retail store or bank.

For most employed people, especially those who commute and work in corporate America, they earn their wages based on a week that consists of forty hours, Monday through Friday. During this timeframe, their workdays usually start between eight and nine in the morning and end somewhere between four and five in the afternoon.

There is also a daily routine of going to work each day and performing specific tasks on the job. Their schedules and workloads are usually decided for them by their supervisor or manager. They do this, day in and day out, and get into a routine that becomes automatic—a habit.

Millions of people have this same routine day after day, month after month, and then—before they know it—years have gone by. It becomes routine without thinking anything about it. So what does this scenario have to do with you as a self-employed individual or sales professional?

My point is that many new entrepreneurs do not have the self-discipline or time-management skills to properly manage their day. It had basically been done for them without their realizing it. They had not made their own hours or designed their workday around what they wanted to do. They also typically had not controlled the ebb and flow of the day-to-day business transactions of the company. It had been done for them. Their job descriptions typically had not entailed buying, selling, and marketing products and services; managing cash flow and expenses; and worrying about whether or not the company was profitable while they had been earning their paycheck.

Why stop your daily routine once you become self-employed? Is it because you are now your own boss and you can choose how many hours or how often you want to work? Yes. It is—as long as you are making the amount of money that you want to make. But if you are not making the money you are accustomed to making or it's insufficient to cover both your personal and business expenses, the answer is likely that you have made a poor management decision and now need to get back on track and in a routine. Once you do, it will become a habit, and you will enjoy much more success that will hopefully turn into more revenue for you. The key to success is discovering which habits are necessary for you in order to reach your goals. The key is as unique as you are.

Are You an Exceptional Employee?

All of us would like to believe that we are ideal employees, but some of us would admit that, regrettably, we are not. Some people take it as a badge of honor that they "screwed" over their employers. If you are one of these people, just stop reading because there is not much hope for your success as an entrepreneur. You don't have the right attitude for being your own boss, because being your own boss requires discipline, which you lack. Think of it as being in the military. Those that enlist don't get to do what they want to do when they want to do it, right? Why should that be any different in the corporate world?

I have read many books that talk about how poorly workers are treated, have heard about it so many times, and—quite frankly—there have been quite a few situations in which I felt as if I have been mistreated. When I look back on them, I see that, most of time, I could have avoided the trouble if I had initially done things differently. Coming from both the employee and employer perspectives, it often comes down to a difference of opinions or a lack of communication between the parties involved. Now, I'm not saying that there aren't some terrible work environments, that there are no glass ceilings, or that there are not bad employers, because I have been in one or two of those situations myself.

A successful entrepreneur is typically a previously conscientious employee and one who met and exceeded the expectations of the employer. Let me give you an example of this. I spent twenty-six years in the mortgage industry and was fired two times in my career. I deserved one of those firings but did not deserve the second one. I was divested both times and licked my wounds and recovered. I had no choice but to recover quickly since I was a single mother with two children under the age of four. These experiences changed my life. It was then that I decided never to rely on anyone else for deciding whether I was worthy of a job or living up to someone else's expectations. I was going to exceed everyone's expectations because I was never going to be humiliated by another person that I worked for again. In order to do this, I had to set my standards very high. I was determined that I would excel at everything that I tried. I had no fear of failure. I saw failure solely as a mean to an end.

Do You Have the Employee Mentality?

Ask yourself these questions and answer truthfully.

- Do you need a structured environment to be productive?
- Are you a good time manager?
- Are you a self-starter?
- Do you prefer working nine to five, Monday through Friday?
- Is each workday planned out?

- Do you return e-mails and phone calls promptly?
- Do you have excellent customer service skills?
- Are you just interested in earning a paycheck and going home?

If you work to just to earn a paycheck and there is no desire to exceed expectations and excel in the workplace, then perhaps you may not be a good business owner. It is my belief that people who want to excel at everything they do usually have the drive, determination, and ambition to run a business. People who just go to work year after year to do nothing more than earn their paychecks are usually not self-motivated and ambitious. Not everyone is cut out to be an entrepreneur. There's nothing wrong with that. Again, you must decide whether you want to be a worker bee or the queen bee.

If you answered yes to needing a structured work environment to be productive, that could be a positive attribute, because you do not work well in chaos, and—typically—not many things can be accomplished in a disorganized workplace. However, if you cannot self-manage your day or your work environment, you may not be self-motivated. If you are not a self-motivated individual, you may have a difficult time with time management. Looking for others to motivate you is not a particularly good quality to have. Successful entrepreneurs do not rely on others to motivate them; they are motivated by ambition and by achieving success for themselves.

Successful business owners must have excellent time-management and customer-services skills. They also understand that providing excellent service to their customers will propel them to greater success in running a business.

"You've got to know what you want. This is central to acting on your intentions. When you know what you want, you realize that all there is left then is time management. You'll manage your time to achieve your goals because you are clear."

- Patch Adams

TIME MANAGEMENT

CHAPTER 7
TIME MANAGEMENT

Ask certain people about managing time, and they conjure up dreaded images in their minds of a person with a twenty-item to-do list, clutching her Day-Timer or smartphone filled with appointments.

Sometimes people who pride themselves on efficiency are merely busy. In their rush to check off items on their to-do lists, they may be fussing over things that don't matter—tasks that create little or no value in the first place. The point to managing time is not to load ourselves down with extra obligations. Instead, the aim is to get the important things done and have a life. An effective time manager is a person who's productive and relaxed at the same time.

Personal style plays an important role as well. Left-brained people thrive on making lists, scheduling events, and handling the details first. This may not work for people who like to think visually. There are as many different styles for managing time as there are people. The trick is to discover what style works best for you. If you need a daily routine to manage your time, set a time schedule that will work best for you, and stick to it. Start your workday the same each day and end it the same time each day. This will help you maintain a balance between work and your personal life.

Try to avoid overscheduling your day and/or week. The point is to manage your time wisely so that you are productive and to schedule downtime after normal business hours. Business hours should be spent on business, not on personal time. If entrepreneurs would discipline themselves as it had been done *for* them during their time in the corporate world, I believe they would achieve more success. Your time for family, friends, and personal activities should be planned for after normal business hours. After-work hours and weekends should be used for errands, family time, and relaxation and for getting chores done around the house.

Tips on How to Manage Your Time

Know Your Limit

Begin managing time from a bigger picture. Consider what that expanse of time is all about. Write a short mission statement for your life: a paragraph that describes your values and the kind of life that you want to lead. Periodically, stop to think about how what you're doing is contributing to that life you want.

Do Less

Managing time is as much about dropping worthless activities as it is about adding new ones. The idea is to weed out activities that deliver little reward.

Remember People

Few people on their deathbeds ever say, "I wish I'd spent more time at the office." They're more likely to say, "I wish I'd spent more time with my family and friends." The pace of daily life can lead us to neglect the people we cherish. Efficiency is a concept that applies to things, not people.

Focus on Outcomes

You might feel guilty if you spend two hours napping or watching TV, but if you're regularly meeting your goals and leading a fulfilled life, there's no harm done. When managing time, it's the overall goal of effectiveness that counts more than the means you use to get there.

Handle It Now

A backlog of unfinished tasks can result from postponing decisions or procrastinating. An alternative is to handle the task or decision immediately. It's better to graciously say no to projects that you do not need to take on. Be careful not to overcommit yourself.

Forget about Time

Schedule "downtime" every day—a period when you're accountable to no one and have nothing to accomplish. This is the time to feel no guilt. A few minutes spent this way each day can yield a sense of renewal.

"By the way, intelligence to me isn't just being book-smart or having a college degree; it's trusting your gut instincts, being intuitive, thinking outside the box, and sometimes just realizing that things need to change and being smart enough to change it."

- Tabatha Coffey

WHAT DOES "THINK OUTSIDE OF THE BOX" REALLY MEAN?

CHAPTER 8

WHAT DOES "THINK OUTSIDE OF THE BOX" REALLY MEAN?

This is one of the most overused phrases that I have come across in business. Yes, we all know what it means, but are we creative enough and willing to take risks to move out of our comfort zones? Those who are the most financially successful have not only done so but have challenged themselves to remove habitual thinking from their daily lives.

Just because everyone else you know is doing it one way does not mean it is the right way. I read a story about Roger Bannister, the first human to ever run a mile in less than four minutes. He did this in 1964, and this had been considered an impossible feat as far back as when Greek runners were tied to horses to make them run faster. Within a month of this phenomenal feat, another man ran a mile in under four minutes, and within a year, twelve others accomplished it as well. The moral to this story is that Roger Bannister broke the mold for habitual thinking.

People who think outside of the realm of normal thinking and who are not so concerned with conforming and following what everyone else does are the true innovators of the world. Those who dare to challenge the trend are those who achieve the most success.

"People may hear your words, but they feel your attitude."

- John C. Maxwell

ATTITUDE

CHAPTER 9

ATTITUDE

Having a negative attitude will make or break your career and will interfere with your business success. Often, I run across people who believe that they are positive people. If they are asked whether the glass is half full or half empty, they will always answer, "It's half full." It's no further from the truth than is "the sky is always blue."

Often, we really do not know how people perceive us. We can be completely clueless. After six months of networking, if you are not getting any referrals from the networking organizations that you are actively involved in, you need to reevaluate the situation. Ask your accountability partners or people whom you trust in business to share how they perceive you. You may be surprised by their comments, especially if they run counter to how you perceive yourself. Take constructive criticism as a gift; do not take it personally.

*A positive attitude may not solve all your problems, but it
will annoy enough people to make it worth the effort.*

— HERM ALBRIGHT, QUOTED IN READER'S DIGEST, JUNE 1995

If you wake up in the morning not feeling well, it is amazing how your
mind-set can change how you feel both physically and mentally. You always
have a choice as to how you want to feel, both positively and negatively.

"Too often in life, something happens and we blame other people for us not being happy or satisfied or fulfilled. So the point is, we all have choices, and we make the choice to accept people or situations or to not accept situations."

- Tom Brady

THE BLAME GAME

CHAPTER 10
THE BLAME GAME

The test of character is not to blame everyone else for your failures. Accept responsibility for your mistakes and don't go looking for people at whom to point the finger. This requires a great amount of discipline because the easiest thing for all of us is to blame someone else. Reevaluate the organizations that you are involved in, your approach to people, and whether you are more on the giving or the receiving end.

When people belong to networking organizations, they often blame the organization for their lack of success when, in reality, it may be something as simple as not being a good fit for the organization. Sometimes there is an oversupply of industries represented, their products or services may not be in demand, or they could be overpriced. Many people believe that if they simply show up for each meeting, they have earned the business. That is not reality.

Ultimately, we are responsible for ourselves and the decisions that we make. If any situation or circumstance is not working for you, move on, reevaluate, and change your plan of action.

"Really good customer service will deliver sales. You are training salesmen to give the best possible advice and then to achieve the sale. People actually like you to ask for a sale because it shows you value their business."

- John Caudwell

WHAT HAPPENED TO CUSTOMER SERVICE?

CHAPTER 11
WHAT HAPPENED TO CUSTOMER SERVICE?

S ome of us who have been around for generations remember the days when the only communication was by telephone and the US Postal Service. In those days, customer service was defined by politeness, courtesy, and respect. I find it remarkable that I am devoting a whole chapter to customer service, but I have found that customer service actually does not mean what it used to mean. The new generation of people, born in the era of technology with texting, do not understand the importance of communicating face-to-face or in a way that another person would prefer to communicate. None of us should make the assumption that all parties want to communicate as we choose to communicate.

First there was e-mail, and now we have text messaging. I am often confounded as to why some business owners either choose to ignore all methods of communication or rely on only one method in order to communicate. For example, those who prefer texting and are consumed by it, have a tendency to ignore their e-mail and telephone calls. Those who love e-mail tend to ignore their phone calls. Those who prefer the phone ignore their e-mail. Forget about what your personal preference is; it's not about you; it's about how the prospective customer wants to communicate with you.

If you do not check your e-mail every day, then have an auto reply stating that you will be out of the office and will reply to e-mail within forty-eight to seventy-two hours. Your reply should also state that if information is needed sooner, please text your message to your phone number or call and leave a voice mail.

Regardless of how busy and overwhelmed you feel, by ignoring a person's attempt at reaching you, you are conveying the message that the person's phone call, e-mail, or text is not important to you. Ask yourself: Is this how you want to treated? Remember the golden rule: do unto others as you would have them do unto you.

> In the corporate world, no monitoring is done until someone complains. You work at your own pace. In the world of the business owner, no one complains; they just don't call back.

There are still some of us who expect our phone calls, e-mails, and text messages to be returned in a timely manner. Now, that brings up another question: What is considered timely? As a rule of thumb, twenty-four hours from the time that you received the call unless it's an emergency situation. If this is not possible, be sure to state this on your out-of-office reply. If you are in a time-sensitive industry, you should hire temporary help and plan in advance to give them adequate training to cover most situations when you will be out of the office. The question is: Should you expect people to wait on you to do business? A reasonable answer would be no.

The reality is that people couldn't care less if you need a vacation or you have sick children. They expect business owners to act like business owners and have procedures in place to handle emergencies. It would not be reasonable to expect your customers to wait for you to return from vacation before they receive service. Imagine Microsoft being "closed" while Bill Gates was on vacation.

"Your mind, while blessed with permanent memory, is cursed with lousy recall. Written goals provide clarity. By documenting your dreams, you must think about the process of achieving them."

- Gary Ryan Blair

Why Writing Down Your Goals Is So Important

CHAPTER 12

WHY WRITING DOWN YOUR GOALS IS SO IMPORTANT

I f you write down your goals, they are no longer abstract to you. You can constantly remind yourself of what you are trying to achieve, and—most importantly—you can plan your action toward that end. You must clearly define your goals and define the path of reaching them by laying out a well thought-out plan. Failing to plan is planning to fail.

In a *Wall Street Journal* article written by Sharon Hadary, former executive director and founder of the Center for Women's Business Research stated that the number one determining factor for a business's success is goal setting. She wrote that "the value of setting high goals for growth is not just a motivational myth. Research shows that the only statistically significant predictor of business growth is not the industry, size of business or length of time in business. It is the entrepreneur's goal for growth."

You must have the right mind-set to chart a plan to achieve your goals. Setting a specific goal leads to better performance when compared to setting an abstract goal (e.g., "I'm going to get a ninety-five percent on my next exam," versus "I'm going to do my best on my next exam.").

Every business owner should set goals, and every company that has achieved any measure of success has had goals. People need to continually set new goals in order to maximize their full potential.

Achieving Success Requires Measuring It

1. **A goal must be written down.**

   The process of writing down our goals forces us to transform our vague desires into concrete objectives.

2. **A goal must be specific.**

   Specific goals help us focus our energy and make the most of how we spend our time. Rather than saying, "I want to make my life better," set specific goals, such as, "I want to purchase a convertible or a house in Beverly Hills," or "I want to make three million dollars."

3. **A goal must be measurable.**

   If our goals aren't measurable, how will we know when we've reached them? An example of a measurable goal is: "I want to lose fifteen pounds," instead of just "I want to lose weight."

4. **A goal must have a time frame.**

    We must put our goals in terms of time; otherwise, we might put them off indefinitely. The time frame for one of your goals could be anywhere from one week to ten years or more. The important thing is to have a deadline—and stick to it!

"If you go to work on your goals, your goals will go to work on you. If you go to work on your plan, your plan will go to work on you. Whatever good things we build end up building us."

- Jim Rohn

SCIENCE SUPPORTS
GOAL SETTING

CHAPTER 13

SCIENCE SUPPORTS GOAL SETTING

From a scientific research perspective, goals serve as a directive function, they have an energizing effect, and they influence persistence and action.

Studies show that specific, difficult goals consistently led to higher performance than did urging people to "do their best." In short, when people are asked to do their best, they do not do so. This is because "do-your-best" goals have no external reference, allowing for a wide range of acceptable performance levels, which is not the case when a specific goal set. On the other end of the scale, creating unattainable goals can cause performance anxiety.

Self-Confidence as It Relates to Goal Setting

Psychologists have found a variety of interactions between confidence in completing a task (self-efficacy) and goal setting:

"The concept of self-efficacy is important in goal setting theory in several ways. When goals are self set, people with high self-efficacy set higher goals than do people with lower self-efficacy. They also are more committed to assigned goals, find and use better task strategies to attain the goals, and respond more positively to negative feedback than do people with low self-efficacy" (Locke and Latham 1990; Seijts and B. W. Latham 2001).

Goal Commitment

According to Locke and Latham, the goal-performance relationship is strongest when people are committed to their goals. Two key factors affect goal commitment: (1) the importance placed on attaining the goal and (2) belief that the goal can be attained (self-efficacy).

Feedback is essential to tracking one's success toward completing a goal.

For goals to be effective, people need feedback that reveals progress in relation to their goals. If they do not know how they are doing, it is difficult or impossible for them to adjust the level or direction of their effort or to adjust their performance strategies to match what the goals require. If the goal is to run three miles in a day, people have no way to tell if they are on target unless they know where the three-mile marker is. When people find they are below target, they normally increase their effort or try a new strategy.

> High goals lead to greater effort than do low goals.

"Set your goals high, and don't stop till you get there."

- Bo Jackson

WHAT THE SALES EXPERTS SAY ABOUT GOALS

CHAPTER 14
WHAT THE SALES EXPERTS SAY ABOUT GOALS

What do the most successful sales professionals say about goal setting?

Brian Tracy

Brian Tracy is an international motivational speaker with an amazing philosophy. He has consulted for more than one thousand companies and addressed more than five million people in five thousand talks and seminars throughout the United States, Canada, and fifty-five other countries.

This is what he says about goal setting:

"Your ability to set goals and make plans for their accomplishment is the "master skill" of success. The development of this ability and you're making it a lifelong habit will do more to assure high success and achievement in your life than any other skill you can possibly learn.

As with anything, you only *own* the process of goal setting by learning it and then by applying it over and over until it becomes automatic, like breathing in and breathing out. Your goal must be to become a continuous goal setter. You must become so clear and focused about what it is you want that every single hour of every day you find yourself doing things that are moving you in the direction of your own choosing."

Zig Ziglar

Zig Ziglar was a master at motivating people, and he started his career as a champion seller of products and services. Ten of his twenty-five books have been best sellers. His famous quotes have been coined by many successful sales professionals.

"There is no way around the fact that a person must master the skill of goal setting if he or she wants to scale the lofty heights all great achievers have climbed. There's a good reason for that. Because when you are effective at goal setting, you will:

- Achieve more and increase your motivation to achieve
- Increase your pride and satisfaction in your accomplishments
- Improve your self-confidence
- Eliminate attitudes that hold you back and cause unhappiness."

Tom Hopkins

Tom realized that selling is a learned skill. By the time he turned twenty-seven, he was a millionaire salesperson in real estate. He set records that remained unbroken until this century. In his last year as a real estate agent, he sold 365 homes—the equivalent of one each day. In total, he closed 1,553 real estate transactions in a period of six years.

Tom Hopkins has been recognized as America's number one sales trainer and the "Builder of Sales Champions." The US Army, Best Buy, AFLAC, and State Farm are some of the two hundred-plus companies Tom has trained.

"To accomplish anything in life, it helps if you have some idea of what you want as the result of your actions. That's called setting a goal. The whole purpose of setting goals is to plan your life rather than take life as it comes. The most important part of goal setting is knowing what it is you want. Once you decide what that is, write it down! After you have written your goals down, keep them somewhere where you can see them daily. As you achieve each one, add another."

"Setting goals is the first step in turning the invisible into the visible."

- Tony Robbins

DEFINING WHAT YOUR GOALS SHOULD BE

CHAPTER 15
DEFINING WHAT YOUR GOALS SHOULD BE

Ask yourself what you want in life. Are you setting goals that are reasonable and attainable based on your commitments to yourself or to your family? How badly do you want to achieve them? Most of all, don't lie to yourself when setting your goals. Set goals that *you* want to accomplish, not goals that others want to set for you. Goals should be yours and only yours!

Sales professionals are often given goals that are preset by their employers. These goals are based on what the average salesperson is doing within the company in an average timeframe. If you are not able to manage those goals within a set timeframe, the employer will either reevaluate you to determine if you need lower goals and/or a longer time frame to accomplish the set goals, or he will simply determine that you are not a good fit for the organization.

If you were to hire a professional salesperson for your company, what would be the defined goals that you would set forth and in what timeframe? Now, at the end of that timeframe, what would you do if the salesperson had not achieved the goals that you had set forth? Which course of action would you take?

If you said that you would dismiss this employee, would you be willing to fire yourself?

What's the Basis for Your Goals?

In order for you to make as much money as *you* want to make, you must know how many sales *you* need to make to generate *your* revenue stream, and you must be able to measure it. Knowing your closing ratio will help you determine how many calls you need to make to meet your sales goals.

Knowing exactly what you need to make is important in order for you to determine how many units of your product or service that you need to sell. Once you know how many units you need to sell each week for your monthly goal, you can determine your closing ratio.

What is a closing ratio? It's the number of calls or contacts that you need to make to sell one unit.

Need versus Want

If it is income, use this calculation: how much income you need to make monthly, divided by the cost of your product or service, equals the number of units you must sell each month. Let's work off of gross figures, as if you were earning an equivalent salary with someone else.

Example: You **need** to make $60,000 a year. The average retail price for your product is $275.00; net after expenses equals $137.50. You would need to sell thirty-six units each month to earn just under $5,000 of monthly gross income, or 432 units annually (36 units x 12 = 432 units)

Goals Based on What You *Want*

You *want* to make a $100,000 annually. The average retail price of your product is $275.00. Your net profit of your goods sold after expenses are $137.50. You will need to sell sixty-one units each month, which equates to 727 units per year.

Tips to Achieving Your Goals

You must have a plan in order to achieve it. Plan, plan, plan!

Written Daily Plan—What are the day's "must do" tasks? Prioritize your tasks. You should know what you want to accomplish on a daily basis. Quit winging it. Procrastination will occur if you have no specific plan for the day. Have daily goals to meet. "I am going to make three sales calls per day. I am going to attend one networking meeting per week."

Accountability Partners—Stay in touch with the people who will hold you accountable and keep you focused. These are typically not your friends or family. It should be people with similar goals to yours. Sometimes family and friends may be too critical or at least not impartial.

Circles of Influence—Regular conversations and/or meetings are important to develop the relationships to build referrals. You must reciprocate and pay it forward. Spend time with people who have similar goals to yours.

Business Networking—You should regularly attend meetings, commit to organizations that you like, and invest in the organizations and its members.

Prospecting—This is a continuous task. You should view everyone you meet as a potential customer or source of referrals.

Cold Calling—This is necessary if you do not build relationships with the people you meet while networking. Think of it this way: every time you meet a new person, this is a cold call that becomes a warm call.

Relationship Selling (Marketing)—This is an ongoing activity of calling on a person in your target market over a period of time in order to earn the person's trust.

In today's market environment, relationship marketing and selling is the most common way to achieve results and financial success. It sometimes takes longer, and it requires more patience!

"I believe the target of anything in life should be to do it so well that it becomes an art."

- Arsene Wenger

DEFINE YOUR TARGET MARKET

CHAPTER 16
DEFINE YOUR TARGET MARKET

What Exactly Does "Target Market" Mean?

Defining your target market is crucial to your success. I once had a member of my business networking organization who sold mobile phone advertising. At the time, mobile phone advertising was new to the market, and there was not much statistical data supporting the effectiveness of this type of advertising. It's usually very expensive, and the customer or potential customer must opt-in in order for you to send advertising to their mobile phone. While the use of mobile texting is extremely popular, it is not used by all age groups. The question is: Will this type of marketing capture your target market? Understanding your target market is crucial before spending money on marketing. Many times, business owners waste money by marketing to the wrong groups.

Determine who will want your product and service and who can afford it. If you are selling baby clothes, your product most likely will not be accepted in the business networking community. Find groups who meet and cater to stay-at-home moms or moms with home-based busi-nesses and young children.

Knowing Your Target Market Is Important

Study your market inside and out.

When I ask people what their target market is, they typically reply, "Everyone is my target market." Next, I ask them, "How do you plan to market to everyone?" Very few people have a clue about what I am asking. The truth is, you rarely can be all things to all people. If your customer base is so broad, how do you plan to market to the whole world? How can you afford to market to the whole world? When will you have the time? Do you have the financial means to market to an undefined market?

As much as we all want to believe that everyone wants or needs our product or service, that's not usually the situation. Defining your ideal target market will save you a lot of time and money. Do some research on the Internet about your products and services. Learn as much as you can about your competitors. Examine what is currently happening in your industry, and then look at what is specifically happening within your target market.

Ask yourself: *What am I doing to stay current with the trends in my industry? How will these trends affect my target market?*

In order to anticipate the trends in your industry, you need to study and stay current with what's happening in it. The best thing that you can do is become the target market's "go to" person. Be the expert everyone goes to for information and resources.

Remember Your Current Customers

Deliver what your customers need and want. Listen to your customers and provide extraordinary products and customer service. The successful and innovative businessperson is a great listener. Being a great listener and asking well-crafted, open-ended questions go hand in hand. The best way to learn more about what your customers want or need is to talk to them and market to them directly based on what you learn from them.

It's not about what *you* want or need; it's more about what other people want and need. Take the time to look and listen to what your ideal customer is saying about his or her current and future expectations. Become an innovator in your industry!

Ask yourself: *How can my products and services solve a problem or fill a need or desire?*

Being an innovator means thinking out of the box and making your own opportunities. Listening to your customers amounts to doing your homework and providing yourself with a firsthand impression of the industry and your ideal customer.

Listen carefully and discover what need or expectation is not being filled within your target market and figure out a way that *you* can fill this void better than anyone else.

Get Acquainted with Your Competition

Fearing competition or avoiding it reflects a lack of confidence in yourself and what you are selling. One of the best ways to get acquainted with your competition is to network with them; don't avoid them. If you are aware of how your competitors are marketing themselves, then you have a greater opportunity to know how to counter-market yourself. Be sure to understand the differences between your and your competitors' benefits and be able to explain the differences.

Don't be afraid of friendly competition. If you avoid it, you will never be able to sell against it. Knowing as much as possible about your competition could be beneficial to you. Typically, your competition is only selling the positive benefits of their products or services. You can point out the differences and overcome any weaknesses of your competitors if you know what they are. Most importantly, you can learn what your product strengths are against your competitors as well as the weaknesses that will help you overcome objections from your prospective customers.

"If human beings had genuine courage, they'd wear their costumes every day of the year, not just on Halloween."

- Douglas Coupland

THE LIKEABILITY FACTOR

CHAPTER 17

The Likeability Factor

Most of us do business with people we like and trust. It's human nature to do business with people we like. Con artists are likeable people, too. If you are networking, and this is the main route you choose to market your product, you must be likeable. Being shy, passive, and withdrawn is not going to win you many referrals. This is where you *must* reach outside of your comfort zone. Taking the initiative to connect with people is crucial to your success.

Be authentic and genuine. People can sense when others have an alternative motive or are insincere. I have met many people who were active in networking and did not get much business from the networking group. People who are likeable, however, are sought out by other people. If you are never one of those people who others seek out, you need to determine the reason people are not drawn to you. Ask yourself: When you seek attention, do you seek it to draw attention to yourself or for the purpose of helping someone else?

Sometimes people may be intimidated or threatened by you because of your confidence—something that they lack. If you are shy, people may interpret your shyness as being snooty. If you are overbearing, people will withdraw from you. Find a good balance between being confident and reserved.

"Figure out what you're good at and start helping other people with it; give it away. Pay it forward. Karma sort of works because people are very consistent. On a long enough timescale, you will attract what you project."

- Naval Ravikant

PRACTICE WHAT YOU PREACH

CHAPTER 18
PRACTICE WHAT YOU PREACH

P eople dislike a hypocrite. If you state that you provide great customer service, provide great customer service. You will get more referrals from your customers if you do. This means returning calls and e-mails or any other form of communication promptly.

If you state that you are reliable and dependable, honor your commitments. Do not expect any more from other people than what you are willing to give.

Gratitude

> Gratitude—it's not enough to feel it. We've got to express it
> because unexpressed gratitude communicates no gratitude at all.
> —*AUTHOR UNKNOWN*

This is one characteristic that I find people lack most. The world would be a better place if people expressed their gratitude publicly and more often, especially in business. I believe those who frequently express their gratitude, regardless of how small the gesture is, are generally happier people.

Pay It Forward

Just about everyone has heard the words *pay it forward*, and most of us understand what it means. But how often do we practice paying it forward? Probably more often than we know, but I have found that that *paying it forward* is a lot harder to practice in a business environment. It's natural for all of us to want something in return.

If you know how to help someone or have the ability to help someone, the right thing to do is to help them without asking for anything in return. The more that you can do this in practice, the more rewarding it can be for you. In the movie *Pay It Forward*, the main character had to carefully decide who he helped before he would go out and *pay it forward*. Like the character in the movie, you may be disappointed with the outcome, but understand *that paying it forward* cannot always be measured.

The Art of Reciprocation

Taking business for granted can quickly drive it away. People want to feel appreciated, and whenever you can, you should reciprocate. You may not have the financial means to reciprocate in kind, but the opportunity to refer business to another person should always be in the forefront of your mind.

In today's marketplace, people have more choices available to them than ever before. Don't assume that you deserve anyone's business unless you have truly earned it. Even if you have earned it, set up some sort of system in which you acknowledge those who have been a good source of referrals or repeat customers.

"You never get a second chance to make a good first impression."

- Author unknown

First Impressions—Just How Important Are They?

CHAPTER 19

First Impressions—Just How Important Are They?

T he first impression could be their only impression of you. If it is not favorable, then they may tune you out. Experts believe that in the first four seconds, people will make judgments about you and tell themselves:

- I will (or will not) buy from this person
- I will (or will not) like this person
- I find this person kind (or not)
- I find this person intelligent (or not)

Some people put very little time into their appearance—and it shows. Good grooming and ensuring that your clothes fit properly are necessary in order to appear credible and respectable. Looking good gives you confidence. Sometimes, personality can overcome bad first impressions, but, most often, people are not given a second chance to impress. Sometimes conforming to standard business attire is required to earn the respect of the person you are seeking to sell your products to.

Not only is your appearance important, but your place of business can reflect negatively on you as well. Assuming that it does not matter to other people is a huge mistake. Let me share a story with you.

In my networking organization, I had a very talented photographer who worked out of her house. She had been a member for months and photographed many of the members for their professional headshots. I hired this photographer to shoot the cover of a magazine that we were publishing at the time. It was a group picture, and when I was scheduling this with those in the group, I had several of the members ask me if I had ever been to her home. I had not, and most had assumed that I had. Their concerns and complaints for having the shoot at her home were that it was cluttered, dirty, and had a distinct odor from her pets.

At that time, all those who were involved disclosed to me that they were extremely pleased with her work but could not recommend her or refer customers to her, because they believed it would cast a poor reflection on them by doing so. This is a case where first impressions did matter and halted any opportunity for this person to get repeat business and referrals.

People are too embarrassed to be honest and prefer not to address their true feelings sometimes. For that reason, don't be oblivious to your surroundings. Check your competitor's workplace or make arrangements to meet people in other locations if you cannot maintain a professional image within your home.

Do not make the critical mistake of assuming that appearance does not matter to people.

"Optimism is the faith that leads to achievement. Nothing can be done without hope and confidence."

- Helen Keller

BUILDING CONFIDENCE

CHAPTER 20

BUILDING CONFIDENCE

C onfidence is your greatest selling tool! Without the right amount of confidence, people will see right through you. Confidence comes from knowing your product and service inside out and feeling good about you.

Having the right amount of confidence is important because too much confidence can convey arrogance. Gaining confidence takes practice and skill. It's about doing things outside of your comfort zone, meeting diverse people, learning about your competition, understanding your weaknesses, and building on your strengths.

Best Tips on Building Confidence

- Dress professionally and wear clothes that fit well, are best suited for your weight, and are age appropriate.
- Learn what people like the least about you.

- Know what people like the most about you, and accentuate it.
- Practice your elevator speeches—have several and change them frequently.
- Know the best and worst things about your product or service.
- Always maintain good eye contact with people without staring.
- Have a prepared presentation before meeting a prospective client.
- Know as much about the prospective client as you can before meeting her.
- Have a firm, confident handshake: people will judge you on your handshake—it is a fact!
- Know the standard objections that you hear from people about your product and service and practice how to overcome them with your prospective clients.
- Smile, and be friendly.

"Ninety-nine percent of the failures come from people who have the habit of mak-

ing excuses."

- George Washington Carver

NO EXCUSES

CHAPTER 21

NO EXCUSES

I t's very simple: making excuses wastes time, money, and energy. So don't do it. And no one likes a whiner.

The more time you waste on making excuses, the more you'll start believing in them.

Everyone knows that negative energy has a negative impact on everyone around. Have you ever been at a business meeting or function where people scatter like roaches when someone they don't like heads in their direction? Well, that may be a good hint for you if you notice it happening to you. Be careful about becoming a negative person or giving off the wrong vibes.

Positive people get positive results. Making excuses is just another form of procrastination.

Remember, very little is gained by making excuses. Enough said, right? I'm sure that you get the point.

"Every sale has five basic obstacles: no need, no money, no hurry, no desire, no trust."

- Zig Ziglar

"NO" IS OK

CHAPTER 22
"NO" IS OK

I may not like *no*, but I certainly respect it. There comes a time and place where everyone needs to say *no*. It's really OK, because sometimes it's better to say no than to overcommit, fail to comply with an agreement, or provide poor service.

There's nothing worse than being considered unreliable, and—most of the time—the reason that we do not follow through with our commitments is that we have overcommitted or we are concerned about hurting people's feelings. There is always a professional way of telling people no.

Women are especially bad about overcommitting and worrying about hurting people's feelings. It's not something that many of us do well, but if you can learn when it is appropriate to say no in a professional and polite manner, there are two things that typically happen.

First, you will probably gain respect from the other person, and second, you will gain credibility. Practice makes perfect, and if you get really good at saying no politely, you just may be surprised with the results.

"Sometimes, idealistic people are put off the whole business of networking as something tainted by flattery and the pursuit of selfish advantage. But virtue in obscurity is rewarded only in Heaven. To succeed in this world you have to be known to people."

- Sonia Sotomayor

NETWORKING

CHAPTER 23

NETWORKING

T his is the most common method of prospecting because it's what the majority of people prefer to do, and it has become the most acceptable method of developing referral leads. In my opinion, it's because people are uncomfortable with the selling process.

Since this is where most people choose to do most of their prospecting, this is what I am going to spend the most time talking about.

Networking is an important skill to have, so it's important to become proficient at it to help you find the job you desire, climb the corporate ladder, or provide the connections needed in your business.

Choosing a Network Organization

One of the best vehicles to find a suitable networking group or organization is by a referral from someone you know well. Do you respect the person or persons who are recommending the organization, and are they credible sources?

Do you have the same goals that they have? Will your business benefit and will you be able to contribute qualified referrals to other people in the organization?

The Truth about Business Networking

Most of my career has been in B2B sales, and when I first experienced business networking outside the realm of the mortgage industry, I could not believe what I heard. Even though the places and times were different, it always seemed that the same people were traveling to the same places, and saying the same things. I never saw so many rules in my life. It reminded me of being in elementary school. You can't promote yourself; you can't market yourself; and never talk about sales or selling. The experts say that it takes an average of nine months to build a referral source of business. Evidently, most of these people preaching this message never sold a product or service in their life.

OK, do you think that Zig Ziglar, Brian Tracy, Tom Hopkins, and all of those other great salesmen waited nine months to make their first sale or build referrals? Probably not! You would have to be fairly financially sound or have a boatload of money lying around to wait that long before your first referral or sale. Most companies employing commission sales people give them about ninety days to produce some business, or they're usually terminated. So out goes the nine-month rule, doesn't it? Why should the business owner expect less of himself?

Yes, networking is different, and you are there to meet people and not to sell to them. That said, the sales process begins. Keep in mind you are not selling products and services, but you are selling yourself as a reliable, trustworthy, and credible person who is interested in connecting and building relationships in order to become a reliable referral source. In the sales process, regardless of whether you are selling to a consumer or to a business, it's rarely a one-time close. The one-time call approach doesn't have much credibility in the current market. In networking, it's not a one-time close, either. It takes skill and determination to build relationships, but it shouldn't take nine months. If it does, you are doing something wrong, and—of course—you are not going to jell with every-one you meet.

So why can't networking work the same way? It can, but it takes effort and time to make those connections. If it takes most people nine months or longer to get their first referral or sale, because all they are doing is showing up for the meetings and are not connecting outside of those meetings, no wonder it takes that long! Most often people say to me, "I don't have time to meet people on a one-to-one basis." I reply, "Fine. Just expect it to take you longer to get your first referral—if you get one at all." Frankly, I have all the time in the world to get to know people because I like them! I consider it my job to get to know as many people as I can.

Finding the Right Networking Organizations

In order to find the right networking groups or business association, attend a couple of their meetings. Are you welcomed, and does anyone approach you? What's your overall feeling when you are there? Are you comfortable and in your element? Are you included in a conversation when you approach a group? Just because there are a lot of people in attendance does not make it a good referral-based organization. The number of people does not translate directly into referrals. The best way for you to determine if it is a good fit for you is to follow up and connect with the people you met on a one-to-one basis. If they do not reciprocate or seem interested in you, I recommend that you find another organization.

I would use the three strikes rule. Find three people to connect with. If you strike out with the first one, go to the next and keep going. If you have to go beyond three people, again, it's not an organization that holds its members accountable. Be sure you are connecting with members and not guests like yourself because the guests have not made a commitment to the organization. They may be checking it out just as you are. Focus on getting to know the members. You may be able to find member lists on the organizations' websites.

Secondly, what do you need from a networking group? Check out the benefits that the group offers. Do they actively and consistently market all of their members or just a select few? Do you have to pay to get promoted within the organization, such as through sponsorship of an event? How will you be recognized, and can you stand out from the rest of the group? Will your product or service be accepted among the members? Are you a good fit for them? What's important to *you*?

Finally, check out the types of businesses that they are attracting. If the organization has primarily corporate or government businesses represented, is that your target market? Do you have the credibility and the expertise to market and sell to these types of entities? Will they be good referral sources for you, and will you be able to reciprocate? The reason that I point this out is that government agencies and schools are limited with whom they can do business, and it's all done by bidding. If you are a start-up, it's not likely that you will get an opportunity to do business with them, and most importantly, will you be a good referral source for them?

To be successful in networking, you have to be more of a giver than a receiver. I recommend that you focus on two or three networking groups or organizations and commit to all of them. The more time you spend getting to know the regular members, the more success you will have in building your business.

Closed Networking Groups versus Open Networking Groups

First, let me define the difference between the two groups. Closed networking groups or organizations allow only one member per industry to attend or become a member. This means that only one insurance agent who sells property and casualty insurance or one mortgage professional, and so forth, is allowed in the group.

An open networking group does not have limits on the number of people or members who represent an industry to be a part of the organization or group. Everyone has an opportunity to market and promote their business equally, so it comes down to people having the ability to build relationships with a larger group of people.

As a general rule in closed networking, people are trying to avoid competition. In my opinion, it is a weakness to be insecure about yourself or what you are selling. People who choose to network in closed networking groups generally are not as confident, or they are not secure in what they are selling. They like closed networking groups because it gives them comfort that they do not have to compete with someone else providing the same product or service in their group. It's supposed to make everyone including the members of the referral group more comfortable and secure. There are structured to focus on learning what people in the group provide in their weekly meetings. These private groups generally cost more money to join. However, there are exceptions.

Closed networking does have its advantages. For some, not having any competition makes them more confident and secure. It forces people to develop relationships where they may otherwise not make the attempt.

Closed networking groups also have rules in place as well as organized platform structure as well as defined rules, so in order to maintain membership, members must adhere to the rules.

In addition, the focus is on referrals and strictly business without the requirement of building relationships through more social settings.

Civic Organizations

In my experience, these are the best organizations to get involved in and join. The purpose of these organizations is to gather in a group for a common goal: to do good for the community. It's not about gathering for the purpose of self-promotion. Many people who join civic groups are pillars in the community and are very influential in it. Getting to know these people can do more for your business than networking with a bunch of business owners who have the sole purpose of promoting their businesses. It can be a win-win situation: you have the opportunity to help support your community while getting to know some very influential people in it.

The disadvantage with joining these groups is that they require more of a commitment. Meetings are more frequent, and these groups typically require volunteering for their civic projects and mission, all of which requires more of a time investment.

"The aim of marketing is to know and understand the customer so well the product or service fits him and sells itself."

- Peter Drucker

ONE *CAN* BE A LONELY NUMBER

CHAPTER 24
ONE CAN BE A LONELY NUMBER

Don't do it by yourself. So many business owners try to do everything by themselves. This is when the number one truly can be a lonely number. Finding accountability partners and building circles of influence can make the road of entrepreneurship less stressful and keep you motivated to continue with your dreams and achieve your goals. Ask for advice and information from the people you network with, and build relationships with like-minded people, people who have the same goals that you may have in business.

Be careful to avoid people who are not ambitious and are more focused on their personal lives. If you truly want to build your business, and it's not a hobby to you, do not spend time with people who are working their businesses part time. They are not generally as ambitious or driven to succeed in their businesses. It's more to supplement their income or give them some social time outside of their home. Most importantly, do not spend time with people with extreme personal problems. They can bring you down mentally.

Accountability partners are preferably other business owners or professionals who have goals similar to yours. These partners are going to hold you accountable. That's the reason they are called accountability partners! In selecting your partners, you should choose people who make time for you, understand your target market, and are interested in helping you achieve your goals.

Circles of Influence are people with whom you develop mutual business and reciprocal relationships to build referrals. In other words, it's a two-way street. It's about building strong business referrals to help build and grow businesses. The best circles of influence are people you meet through networking organizations who have the same motivations and goals as you have.

In order to be successful in networking, it's important to build relationships within the organizations that you are actively involved with. Choose and interview people you want to get to know in several different networking organizations. Be sure to separate your business life from your personal life.

Consider a business partner. Two is better than one if it's the right partner. You may be able to join forces with another struggling business owner or a profitable one for that matter. Combining resources and sharing in expenses for marketing, or staff can help save your business.

One of the main reasons that businesses fail is that they are usually underfunded. Combining financial resources can eliminate some overhead expenses and help with expanding your businesses.

Collaborating

Collaborating with other businesses is one of the most effective but underused marketing tools that I have ever seen. In a weak economy where customers are few, if business owners collaborated to advertise together, not only would they reduce their advertising costs but they *would* have the opportunity to advertise. So many business owners do absolutely no advertising because they cannot afford it. If strip shopping center owners combined their financial resources to advertise collectively, more people would know that they existed.

How many times have you passed by a building or shopping center and have no idea what businesses were located there? It's not like when you open a business people automatically know that it exists. Do business owners believe that people are driving around looking for new businesses in which to shop?

"I think what I love most about Oprah's brand that I would love to do with the Eva Longoria brand is she has purpose with her brand. Everything she does means something."

- Eva Longoria

LAYERING YOUR MARKETING EFFORTS

CHAPTER 25
LAYERING YOUR MARKETING EFFORTS

Most successful business owners who I have interviewed stated that it usually takes more than one marketing strategy to find their target market and achieve optimum results. It's usually a combination of marketing efforts through trial and error. One universal theme is providing excellent customer service and layering your marketing efforts.

Allocating funds for marketing to drive traffic to your website or directly driving customers to your place of business is necessary in order to expose your business to the buying public. If you are an online company only, it's crucial to have a well-designed website that is search engine optimized (SEO).

Networking is one of the least expensive means to reach an audience, but the problem with networking is you are not reaching the buying public. You are reaching a few people at a time, and networking is based on building relationships for referrals. It does not necessarily equate to direct business.

Social Networking

Everywhere you look, experts tell us that social networking is important—even crucial—to a business. I agree to some extent. In my experience, the only thing that social networking has done for my business is grow the fan base, but it has not generated revenue. Based on my interviews with business owners—those who are very active with social network marketing—they have experienced the same thing. It's mostly the social networking marketing specialists and companies making the statements about how important social networking is, so it is a self-serving purpose.

That said, I do feel that social networking can be valuable by spreading the word about your product and services and developing your brand. If you look at social networking as a branding tool, you have the right perspective. There are always exceptions to the rules.

One important thing that you need to understand about social network marketing is that you must be careful with what you post. It's best to be neutral and not reflect your political and religious views. If you don't mind offending 50 percent of your audience, which may be the best refer-ral source for your business, by all means, go ahead.

Be careful not to leave someone out who has helped you. That includes any networking groups or business associations that you belong to. Each organization is run by someone, and if they notice that you are positively commenting on another organization, it could have a detrimental effect. If you are actively involved in various business organizations, and you actively post on social networking sites, give each organization their fair share of recognition.

Print and Online Advertising

Print and online advertising can be very expensive and should be researched carefully. However, if you are looking to reach a broader audi-ence, advertising in local magazines may be your best alternative. Rarely do you achieve immediate results from any means.

Every publisher of any print or online media will tell you that it takes an average of three to four times for readers to recall and recognize your brand. If you go this route, you need to give it some time.

When you are marketing your business, consider all of these vehicles:

- keyword optimization on your website
- social media marketing

- print and online advertising
- direct mail marketing
- networking
- prospecting and cold calling

"Relationships cannot be made, you are not the creator of things! They are grown, from the seeds of trust, watered with the care of your attitude."

-Wade Harman

BRANDING YOUR BUSINESS

CHAPTER 26
BRANDING YOUR BUSINESS

If you are wondering if branding your business is important, just watch TV for a few minutes, and you will have your answer. Why do companies such as Coke, Pepsi, Chick-fil-A, Budweiser, Wendy's, and McDonald's continue with advertising? They have already branded themselves, and almost the entire global community knows who they are. It's simple: consumers have so many choices these days, and the old saying "out of sight is out of mind" holds true. They want to stay front and center of their customer base.

Think about it for a second. How many times have you been influenced in your lifetime by what you saw on TV, read in a magazine, or heard on the radio? If advertising did not influence the buying public, then corporations would not spend billions annually trying to convince the public to buy their products.

Branding your business is done in everything that you do. The more people who know about your company, the more word-of-mouth advertising you are going to receive. Word-of-mouth advertising is the most effective means of advertising today—and the most cost effective.

If you don't have a business, brand yourself. The more people who recognize and can identify with you will help you build your career regardless of what you decide to do.

"We get wise by asking questions, and even if these are not answered, we get wise, for a well-packed question carries its answer on its back as a snail carries its shell."

- James Stephens

RELATIONSHIP SELLING

CHAPTER 27

RELATIONSHIP SELLING

E very step you take in your business should be about building relationships and about serving your customers in the most effective way. Understand that selling and marketing is *never* about you; it's always about your potential customer. It's about what *they* want, not what you want. They define what is acceptable and what they are willing to pay for it.

If you learn to take your time, be consistent and reliable, and pay it forward as often as you can, you will be surprised just how fast the results will come. When you genuinely take the approach to helping as many people as you can, you *will* get the results that you want. Helping people can be about helping them understand how you can help them with your product or service.

If you choose networking as your main marketing strategy, remember, networking is about getting referrals through relationships. Relationship selling is about selling yourself, not your products and services. Typically, selling your products is frowned upon in networking, and it may negatively affect your chances of getting referrals. People do not like to be sold to, but if they understand how they can help you, they are more likely to do so by referring potential clients. In order to help you, they must clearly understand what you do.

"The propensity to truck, barter and exchange one thing for another is common to all men, and to be found in no other race of animals."

- Adam Smith

You Must Ask

CHAPTER 28
YOU MUST ASK

A t some point in your business or career, you will have to ask for what you want or ask for the business. You can market, run all the ads you want, and network all over the place, but—eventually—you will have to ask someone to buy what you are selling. Unless you are selling iPhones or have invented the next lifesaving product or service, people will not typically be running to you to buy what you are selling.

You must decide which course of action you plan to take in selling your product or service. Are you going to sell to those who you network with, or are you going to find your customers through cold calling and prospecting? No matter which course of action you plan to take, you must ask in order to close the sale.

Once you are confident in yourself and what you are selling, closing will become easier. You will learn to close more sales with practice.

Practice makes perfect. Practicing the art of asking builds confidence, and you become better at asking.

At some point, you must decide that what you are selling is beneficial to others. If you do not believe this, then why are you selling it?

You can sugar coat it all you like, but asking is a step to closing the sale. When you become proficient in asking, you are then rewarded and become satisfied, both financially and emotionally. Results come faster when you believe that you have earned the right to ask.

"Most people will spend more time and energy in going around problems than in trying to solve them. A problem is a challenge to your intelligence. Problems are only problems until they are solved, and the solution confers a reward upon the solver. Instead of avoiding problems, we should welcome them and through right thinking make them pay us profits."

- Henry Ford

BARTERING

CHAPTER 29

BARTERING

Bartering is a multibillion dollar global industry. It's estimated that about one-third of the clients of the oldest bartering company in the world, Atwood Richards, consist of Fortune 500 companies.

This ancient art of trade is making a comeback, especially for small businesses. Bartering has been increasing, and it's estimated that it represents 40 percent of the world's economy. It's said that GE Capital may be doing as much as $15 billion in bartering each year.

So if it's good enough for the big guys, how come it's not good enough for you? The answer lies in education. Some people think that if they barter, they are haggling over price, and they are very uncomfortable with negotiating price. Additionally, many people who have bartered in the past have had bad experiences.

Some may say that there's an art to bartering. Perhaps that's true if you are not very good at negotiating.

My advice is to open your mind to either bartering privately or joining a barter exchange where the negotiation is done for you. There are many benefits to bartering for personal and business reasons.

A good bartering relationship with another party is better than no relationship at all. Often times, bartering allows you to find products and services that you need without spending cash dollars that you don't have. It's also better to have a customer who is willing to work with you than to have no customer at all. One good barter client could provide the potential of dozens of cash business referrals.

Once you have changed your mind-set, learned some new skills and built your confidence, you will be able to negotiate financially sound barter transactions. Practice makes perfect!

My Top Twenty-One Tips for Business Owners and Professional

My Top Twenty-One Tips for Business Owners and Professionals

- Have a purpose, and take action.
- Set goals—plan on how to achieve them.
- Plan each day the day before.
- Don't over book; don't under book.
- Define your target market, and sell to it.
- Promote your company everywhere, including with social media.
- Be professional: return all calls/e-mails promptly.
- Cut expenses and overhead whenever you can.
- Collaborate with other business owners.
- Network and be more selective, but don't over-network.
- Work hard, but be smart about it.
- Manage your time wisely.
- Sell: ask for the business (no one is going to sell your product for you unless you pay them).
- Pay it forward.
- Barter when you can.

- Believe that talking to people can be the best job you ever have!
- Networking is about referrals and *future* sales, not present sales.
- Quit making excuses for things going wrong.
- Get your personal life in order.
- Ask for help!
- Invest in yourself and business—take some risks.

ABOUT THE AUTHOR

About the Author

Being First—Against the Odds

*B*eing first is not easy, especially if it's way out of your comfort zone. Being first, you are taking a risk that perhaps no one else before you has been willing to take. Sometimes being first is about stepping out and being the first to experiment or to innovate. Being first can cause a lot of pressure and stress. You have to like being first.

I was firstborn of two children.

At the age of eighteen, I was the first person in my high school to leave early to go to work after classes. It was years later that other students were allowed to do this.

In 1978, at the age of twenty-three, I was the first female sales agent Metropolitan Life had hired in the district office in Columbus, Georgia. During that era, I was one of the few female agents in the entire company and perhaps in the insurance industry. I had no women role models in sales to mentor me. It was so unusual to have a female sales agent call on businesses in the South, so I was considered much like an anomaly.

Prior to my career in the sales profession, I had no formal sales training and only had a high school education. I went from being a teller in a savings and loan to a sales professional within five years of graduating from high school. Even in today's marketplace, that would be considered unusual and unique.

At twenty-three, I bought my first home. In 1979, a single female in that age bracket represented less than 20 percent of the overall population in the United States for homeownership. I earned enough income in one year from commissions to qualify for an FHA mortgage. I had no cosigner. I was the first in my graduating class in high school to purchase a home. At the time, I didn't know anyone else my age—male or female—who owned a home.

In 1982, four months after my second child was born, as a newly divorced mother, I traveled 228 miles round trip, each day, to work in order to earn enough income to feed, clothe, and shelter my two kids. That's 46,120 miles in nine months.

My day started at five every morning. I dropped my babies off at daycare by six, and I was at work by eight, and after working an eight-hour day, I would head home back to Alabama to pick up my kids by six-thirty in the evening. This exhausting routine went on for almost a year.

Yes, I could have chosen an easier path. I could have chosen to rely on my family to support us or apply for public assistance. For some reason, welfare or government assistance never occurred to me. It was important to me to have accomplishments and achieve financial success by doing it myself. It was never up to my parents to support **my** *family. It was never an option to just get by or to rely on another person to support me and my children. I had to do the right thing by setting an example for them.*

By the time that I was twenty-eight years old, I had owned three homes and had purchased four cars. I was a single mom with two children under the age of five by the time I had bought my third home. My third house was a thirty-five-hundred-square-foot, five-bedroom, three-and-half-bath home with a full-daylight basement in an upper-middle-class subdivision.

In 1992, within three weeks of giving birth to my fourth child, I went back to work in the corporate arena as the sole breadwinner of a family of six.

The moral to my story is that it's all about having the right mind-set to achieve what you want in life. My business success comes down to having an uncanny belief in myself and my abilities, not giving up too quickly—especially when times get tough—making no excuses, and knowing when it's time to reinvent myself. I have failed many times and have picked myself up and started over again.

I have written this book to encourage people to act on their dreams even if it seems scary. It's worth the risk!

Good luck!

www.ingramcontent.com/pod-product-compliance
Lightning Source LLC
Chambersburg PA
CBHW032303210326
41520CB00047B/918